I0151547

GEORGE

The Handcart Boy

by Howard R. Driggs

SOUTHERN UTAH UNIVERSITY PRESS

Cedar City, Utah

Reproduction of
George the Handcart Boy
by Howard R. Driggs
published by the Southern Utah University Press

Front cover coloring by Audrey Corbridge
Redesign by Marissa K. Gifford

ISBN Number Soft Cover: 978-0-935615-34-0
ISBN Number Hard Cover: 978-0-935615-35-0
Library of Congress Control Number 2011941185

GEORGE

The Handcart Boy

by Howard R. Driggs

Illustrated by J. Rulon Hales

ALADDIN BOOKS

New York: 1952

ALADDIN BOOKS IS A DIVISION OF
AMERICAN BOOK COMPANY

COPYRIGHT, 1952, BY HOWARD R. DRIGGS. All rights reserved.
No part of this book protected by the above copyright may
be reproduced in any form without written permission of
the publisher. FIRST EDITION

PRINTED IN THE UNITED STATES OF AMERICA

To
MARGARET, MY WIFE,
*whose authorship has brightened
every part of this true story of
the OLD WEST*

Contents

Dreams of a New Homeland

"WE'RE GOING TO AMERICA! Going to America!"

George Harrison, a lad of twelve, had run all the way home from the big English glass factory in Manchester with the exciting news.

"Is it true, Mother?" asked his younger sister Olive.

"I hope so," replied Mrs. Harrison. "But your father will have to decide."

"He has, Mother!" George exclaimed. "To-day, while we were eating lunch, he said he was through slaving at the smoky old factory."

" 'Does that mean we are taking the ship for America?' I asked him."

" 'Aye, son, the very next boat,' he told me. It made me whistle and jump. No more hard factory work for me! No getting my ears boxed by the boss."

"Has he been hurting you again?" the mother asked tenderly.

"Yes, he slapped me today because a bottle fell from the fork when I was carrying it to the big oven."

"Never mind, Georgie. A warm dinner will help you forget. Go wash the smudge off your face and hands. Alice, set the table. Olive, feed the baby. Father and Aaron and Mary Ann will soon be home from work."

William Harrison, tired from long hours at blowing and shaping bottles, goblets and other glassware, came in. With him were Mary Ann and Aaron.

With clean face and hands, George burst into the room saying, "We're going to America!"

"Hold on, brother," spoke practical Aaron, who was seventeen. "That's a long way from here."

"I know! But a ship will take us across the ocean, and the train will carry us many miles farther, and then we'll soon be in Zion."

"Not so fast," said Aaron. "The missionaries from Utah said there would be more than twelve hundred miles of pulling and pushing handcarts before we get there."

"What are handcarts?" asked little Alice.

"They're like the peddlers' pushcarts that Jerry uses to bring vegetables and fruits to sell us," explained George.

"Yes, but they are larger," added Aaron, "and have higher wheels. Elder Tyler told me all about them. They can carry about two hundred pounds of bedding, clothing and all the other things we'll need on the journey. That will be a mighty heavy load for us to pull and push over the long trail. I wonder if we can do it!"

Mother's call to dinner interrupted the discussion and brought the family promptly to the table. Father Harrison gave thanks and asked the Lord to bless them with love and wisdom, health and courage to carry forward their plan.

It was no sudden decision for the Harrisons. For months after they joined the Mormon Church, they listened to the elders telling about gathering with the Latter Day Saints in Utah —which they felt was Zion. It was founded by the pioneers in the valleys of the far-off Rocky Mountains. They had often sung a hymn written by one of the members, which began—

O ye mountains high, where the clear blue sky
  Arches over the vales of the free,
Where the pure breezes blow, and the clear stream-
    lets flow,
  How I've longed to your bosom to flee.
  O Zion! Dear Zion! land of the free!
Now my own mountain home, unto thee I have
    come—
  All my fond hopes are centered in thee.

While Aaron's clear, rich voice could be heard, it was not with the same zeal as that of the rest of the family. Aaron was as eager as the others to get away from the noisy, dirty iron foundry where he spent ten hours a day for only a few shillings a week. But he couldn't help wondering about the dangers they must face in getting to the Zion of which they dreamed. He decided to question Elder Tyler, one of their Mormon friends. And so one night he asked, "What about the Indians? I've heard they kill and scalp people—even children."

"Well, I've crossed the Plains and mountains several times, my boy," was the reply, "and I still have my hair. I've found Indians are friendly if they are treated fairly. It is usually mean whites that make them act cruelly."

"Are you sure we can make the journey with Mother and the baby?" persisted Aaron. "Are you sure it won't be too hard for them?"

"I'm quite sure. Why, about two thousand folks have already gone through safely," said the Elder. "But we can do it only if we start now and have no bad luck."

"It will take nearly all our savings for the voyage and the train fare," Aaron went on.

"I know it and that is why we are going to use handcarts. They cost less than covered wagons and oxteams. It will save some of your money so that you can get a home and farm in the valleys once you get there," Elder Tyler explained.

"Well, I'm certainly ready to do my part," said Aaron, who, though worried, decided Elder Tyler knew best.

"God bless thee, my son," said Father Harrison. "We'll all do our part and the Lord will take care of us. But we must all pitch in and get everything ready. We must make the next boat, or it will be too late."

"Hooray! We're going to America!" exclaimed George.

"Going to America!" echoed little Alice.

Across the Atlantic

THE TRIP ON THE BOAT was a long and tiring one, but the Harrisons, the Loaders, and about nine hundred other emigrants remained cheerful. And the courage and faith of the officers in the success of their plans kept up the spirits of the more timid among them.

For the children, the days passed quickly. They never tired of watching the great waves that kept the ship rolling.

Porpoises, playing around the ship, thrilled them. Gulls and the other seabirds that followed them far out on the sea, were a continual source of interest. And the day they saw a whale was one never to be forgotten.

"A whale!" shouted George. "A whale!

14

A whale!'' echoed others, dancing up and down.

Just then its head appeared and a spurt of water from the big nose went into the air.

"Why don't they stop the ship and catch the whale?" asked Bob.

"No room on this ship for the big fellow," said the bo'sun. "Besides, we have to get you all to America as quickly as possible."

George and his friend Bob learned all about

the vessel from top deck down to the hold. They made friends with many of the sailors, who didn't object to the lively boys so long as they kept out of the way.

One day George ventured alone into the big kitchen where several fine Negro cooks were getting the meals ready. He watched with interest the way they fried and flipped pancakes.

"Let me try it," he suddenly asked.

"Sure 'nuf, boy. Git dis apern on you, take a flipper and stack 'em up," replied a big cook with a grin.

It wasn't easy at first but soon George learned the trick of pouring the batter, watching till it bubbled, then deftly turning it over. It was fun! And besides, George, who was always hungry, was given some extra food.

Contrary winds drove the *Horizon* some hundreds of miles off course, and the passengers began to worry over the delay.

"Do you think we're going to get to America, Captain?" asked Aaron seriously.

"Any day now," was the smiling answer. "My good ship has never failed."

Sure enough, it wasn't long before the *Horizon* landed them all safely in Boston. And the very next day they started on the long and wearisome journey to Chicago, and then in another smaller train to Iowa City, the capital of Iowa.

All this traveling took time and once again Aaron began to worry. "We keep losing time," he said. "Do you think we can make the journey on to the valleys of the mountains this year?"

"Yes, if we have good luck," said Captain Martin.

But luck had turned against the strangers. The handcarts that had been ordered were not ready. There was nothing to do except pitch camp along the Cedar River and wait. Then, to add to their worries, it began to rain. How it rained!

Morning broke with clear skies. A rainbow added cheer to the drenched camp. "It is our bow of hope and promise," said Father Harrison.

"Hm!" said Aaron. "I'd feel better if I could see some handcarts."

"Amen to that," echoed Sammy Jones, one of Aaron's pals.

Two days later the handcarts began to appear. A few covered wagons, to which oxen were hitched, were also brought into camp. These were to go with the handcart caravan on its long trek west. They were to carry extra supplies. Any who might be ill along the trail would be able to ride in them.

Handcarts West

A TWO-MILE-LONG CARAVAN of handcarts awaited the signal to go. Suddenly "All ready! Start!" came the command from Captain Martin. It was repeated by Lieutenant Tyler and the officers down the line.

As the carts began to roll, everyone sang—

> For some must push and some must pull,
>   As we go marching up the hill;
> So merrily on our way we go,
>   Until we reach the valley, O!
> For some must push and some must pull
>   Before we reach the Valley, O!

People of Iowa City lined the banks of the river to see them start. The caravan was made up of more than two hundred carts, piled high with bedding, food and utensils, about ten covered wagons, and a number of milk cows driven by two boys on ponies.

George and his friend Bob were lucky to be given first chance to ride the ponies. Other boys, willing to stand the dust, would have their turns later. Shep, a dog given to Bob by an Iowa farmer, helped to keep the cattle moving. If any cows lagged, he would nip their heels and hurry them along.

"Hooray! We're on the trail!" shouted George, and Bob echoed his cry.

"Just wait!" Aaron called back. "When you two take turns pulling and pushing, you won't feel so gay."

Father Harrison walked between the shafts of his family handcart and pulled it along while Aaron and Mary Ann pushed. On top of the load, in a cosy nest of pillows, rode the baby. Mother and little Annie walked beside them.

"We'll not go far today," said Lieutenant

Tyler, who rode back and forth along the caravan to cheer the folk. "This is just a 'breaking in' process."

They soon learned what he meant by "breaking in" process. The handcarts, filled with household goods, were not easy to manage. Getting them up a hill was hard work. Getting them down took skill. A top-heavy cart could get out of hand and stage a runaway, finally tipping over with a crash. This happened many times.

The family just ahead of the Harrisons was unlucky enough to have this happen to them. The tired father, who was walking and pulling in the shafts, stumbled and fell. His sons who were pushing, tried to hold back the cart, but the weight of it on the steep hill pulled it away and down the slope it raced, scattering pots, pans, and bedding. Luckily, the cart was not broken. Willing hands soon reloaded it and pushed it back on the trail.

About four o'clock in the afternoon, the

weary pioneers were delighted to hear Captain Martin's welcome command, "Halt; go into camp." The order was passed down the line.

"What a pretty place to spend the night!" said Mother Harrison trying to cheer her tired family.

"It's covered with grass and flowers," said Mary Ann.

"We're lucky that there's plenty of wood to cook our supper," added Aaron.

"And a brook of clear water to help with the cooking and get ourselves cleaned up," said the mother. "Come, little ones, take pails and fill them quickly. But be careful not to tumble into the stream."

"Georgie, go gather wood for the fire," said Father Harrison. "We can all help get the meal. We're hungry and tired from this day's excitement and work, so let's hurry. Thank the Lord no harm has come to us this first day. It is a good omen."

The evening meal—mainly one of "flapjacks" with bacon and warmed-over beans, was eaten with relish. A little molasses, bought at Iowa City, added a touch of sweets.

A bugle call brought all together round a campfire. There was a hymn and prayer. Then Captain Martin spoke:

"We are beginning a long journey. Our start has been greatly delayed, but with the blessing of the Lord, backed by our earnest efforts, we shall see it through. Our rules are few and easy to remember:

"Up at daybreak. Breakfast over and start at six. Keep together for protection. Obey your leaders. Help one another. After supper we'll get together to sing and listen to instructions. Then say your prayers and go to sleep."

Most of them were soon obeying that final word. Sleeping in the fresh air under the stars was wonderful. Sentinels and night herders kept watch over the quiet camp through the summer night.

A bugle call roused the travelers. Sleepy boys felt it had come too early, but up they jumped. Breakfast over, the handcarts were packed. Then with their song, "For some must push and some must pull," gaily ringing out in the clear air, the caravan was again rolling westward over the hills of Iowa.

A few days later they passed the site of what, in time, was to be the great city of Des Moines. Now, there was only a trapper cabin with a few tepees of the Pottawatomie tribe along the river. Father Harrison traded with the friendly Indians, exchanging thread and needles for a small, soft buffalo robe in which to wrap the baby.

Of course the robe was not needed just then, for it was early July and the days and nights were hot. By rising early, the party hoped to make up for lost time, but at best the handcart pioneers could make no more than twelve to fifteen miles a day. And the trip to the mountains was a long one.

It was early August before the caravan reached Council Bluffs on the Missouri River. There they faced another serious problem.

"You are foolish to try to cross the Plains and Rockies so late in the year," said one of the leaders of the town.

"You've more than a thousand miles to travel," added another. "Do some figurin'. If you made fifteen miles a day, it would take you more than two months. And you won't average twelve."

"But what can we do?" worried Father Harrison. "We must have food and shelter if we stay here."

"Scatter out among the Iowa farmers up and down the Missouri valley. They'll be glad to get your help in gathering crops. You can earn enough to winter through."

"Sounds like a sensible plan to me," said Levi Savage.

"I think he's right," said Aaron. "I'm ready to work."

"So am I," spoke up Sam Jones.

"No, no!" said several others. "Let's get on to the valleys. The Lord will help us."

Captain Martin and Lieutenant Tyler listened to all they were saying. Finally, after talking it over, the Captain said, "We will put it to a vote. All who want to go on, raise your right hands."

Only a few voted to stay in Iowa. Most of the band wanted to go on.

"Well, that settles the question," decided the Captain. "Now, let's get across the Missouri into Nebraska without delay."

Ferry boats, loaded with families and handcarts, crossed and recrossed the muddy stream. At Winter Quarters, an all-but-deserted town, the anxious band camped for the night.

Over the Plains

"I'M GOING SWIMMING before I go to bed," said George. "It's just too hot to sleep."

"So am I," said Tom Wilkins. "But where?"

"Why not in the Missouri?" suggested George.

"Just a moment, boys," said Lieutenant Tyler, who had overheard the talk. "The 'Big Muddy' is swift and dangerous. You must keep out of that river."

"Then can we swim in the pond?" asked Tom.

"I wouldn't," was the reply. "Too many mosquitoes in that greenish pond."

"Whose afraid of a few mosquito bites? Come on, Tom," said George.

"All right," said the lieutenant, "but don't tell me afterward that you had no warning."

Into the willows near the pond the boys went and soon they were splashing about. The buzzing insects stung them badly, but the boys cooled off. They felt much better by the time they went back to camp and bed.

"What's the matter with you, Georgie?" asked his mother next morning. "You're all covered with red spots and you look feverish."

"I guess I did wrong last evening," confessed the boy. "Lieutenant Tyler warned us not to go swimming in the millpond."

"Our Tom is in the same fix," spoke up Mrs. Wilkins. "Maybe they've caught the 'chills and fever'—malaria, the doctors call it. They're in for a sick spell if they have."

"And we're in for more pulling and pushing," grumbled Aaron.

By the time the caravan was ready to start, George and Tom were beginning to burn and shiver. They could eat little.

They did not walk that day, nor for ten days afterward. They rode in the covered wagon and how they suffered!

Cooped beneath the canvas, the lads missed the new sights along the trail. Villages of little prairie dogs sitting straight up near their holes and barking sharply at the passersby, amused the children. Prairie chickens scurried by. And sometimes Indian braves, women and papooses on ponies rode past. They laughed and talked about the strange hand-carts.

As the caravan got farther west, the drier air helped George and Tom to get better. Finally they were allowed to walk part of the day. Thin and weak, they had hard work to keep up with the carts and were soon glad to crawl back into the wagons.

"I'll not swim in a pond with mosquitoes again," George said. But then something in the distance caught his attention. "What are those black animals off on the hills?" he asked.

"Buffalo. Oh, look! They're coming toward the handcarts," exclaimed Bob.

Just then Captain Martin and Lieutenant Tyler dashed past on their horses, shouting, "Stop the handcarts! Get your guns, men, and follow us. We must turn the herd or we'll all be trampled!"

Ahead of the caravan the hunters made their stand. As the excited buffaloes neared them, the men began to shoot. Several of the brown leaders of the herd fell and the rest swerved aside enough to miss the handcarts. Away they went toward the Platte River. Right behind them were the Indian hunters who had started the stampede. And lying beside the trail along which they had come were buffaloes they had killed during the chase.

"Let us thank the Lord who has saved us," said Father Loader. "It was a very narrow escape."

"Well, there's one fine thing about it," added Aaron. "We'll have some good meat."

"Swing your carts in a circle," commanded Captain Martin. "We'll camp here."

Several of the men went out to skin and dress the meat of the buffaloes they had killed. Lieutenant Tyler, who had hunted buffalo before this, directed the work. A butcher from Manchester was put in charge of cutting up the meat. Aaron, Sam and the younger men helped to carry the cuts and roasts to the women who, with the help of the smaller children, had "buffalo chip" fires going. How they feasted that night! The meat had come just in time, for the food supply was low.

"Don't overeat," advised one of the leaders. "Too much fresh meat will make you ill."

"I wish we might carry some of it along with us," said Father Harrison.

"By all means do," replied Elder Savage. "But remember that meat spoils quickly in hot weather and, unfortunately, we can't take time to dry any of it."

"Well, the Lord be thanked for giving us a good meal," said Father Loader.

"I hope it isn't the last one on this trip," added Aaron. Well-fed and refreshed by a good night's sleep, they pushed on next morning. George, still weak and shivering, managed to walk several miles beside the cart. Sisters Olive and Alice helped to take his place at the pushing. The load was getting lighter as the food disappeared.

At last the caravan rolled up to Fort Laramie, a soldier post about five hundred miles from the Missouri River. The plains had been crossed, but the mountains still lay before them.

Food was the vital question. It was hoped that a supply of dried buffalo meat might be bought from the Indians. But the Indians would not trade, not even for the pretty cloths, buttons, buckles, thread and other notions the mothers had brought from England.

"We must have food," said Aaron. "I'm going to see what I can get from the soldiers."

And off he went to the supply store where he found the quartermaster.

"We're almost starving—Mother, Father, my sisters and my brother, who is ill," began Aaron. "Here's the last of my savings. Won't you sell us some food?"

"Sorry, boy," replied the soldier, "but we have strict orders not to. We are on short rations ourselves." Then, seeing Aaron's eyes fill with tears, the quartermaster offered a suggestion. "You're a husky young fellow. Why don't you enlist in the United States Army? That would make one less for your father to feed. Besides, if you get in the army, I think I can manage to let you have some extra rations to pass on to your mother and the rest. Think about it, boy."

"Thanks, I will," answered Aaron. Then off he hurried to his father and mother.

"Why, we can't possibly leave you behind," exclaimed his mother.

The sisters began to cry. Olive and Alice

clung to him. George sat by the handcart in tears. Finally Mary Ann spoke. "Aaron, I think you should do whatever seems best."

But all Father Harrison said was, "Let us ask the Lord to guide us in this matter." Quietly they joined him in prayer. Then they consulted Captain Martin, who approved of Aaron's signing up.

So Aaron enlisted. Extra supplies were given them as had been promised and the next morning, Aaron, in uniform, came to see his dear ones off with the handcart caravan.

"God bless and keep thee," said his father.

"And bring you back safely to us," added his mother.

"I'll be in the valleys soon," he answered. "Good luck to you."

"And make it *soon*," called back his pal, Sam Jones.

Patience Loader, oldest daughter of that family, volunteered to take Aaron's place with Mary Ann, at pushing the Harrison cart.

Off with the Indians

"HURRY! HURRY!" became the watchword of the handcart caravan.

"We must get over the Rocky Mountains before snow falls," said Captain Martin.

Everyone who was able helped. George had not regained strength enough to do more than walk, but he was hungry. He was always hungry. There was not enough food to satisfy him. Each person received only a piece of flapjack a day with thin soup and scarcely any meat. The cows gave just enough milk for the little children.

At Deer Creek, about one hundred miles west of Fort Laramie, came an important decision from Captain Martin. "You've done your best," he said, "but we must do even better. Right here, before we move farther, we must lighten our loads so that we can travel faster."

"Why! We have next to nothing left now," said one of the leaders.

"That's true, but, with the exception of food, every single thing that can be left behind must be sacrificed. We must travel as quickly, and therefore as lightly as possible. Bring your extra clothing, quilts, and even treasured articles. Throw them in this pile. You must forget your own feelings. Act now. Here goes my topcoat."

Lieutenant Tyler followed his lead, and others obeyed. The pile in the middle of the camp ground grew.

"Georgie, come here," said Father Harrison. "Go into our tent, take off your worn trousers and put on the new ones the good lady gave you when we were leaving Manchester. Then bring the old pair to me."

The boy obeyed. His father, going carefully

through the pockets, found a piece of rawhide filled with teeth marks. "My poor boy! Have you been so hungry that biting into this has helped?"

"Aye, Father," said George.

Tears filled the father's eyes as he tossed the old trousers into the pile.

Suddenly the boy saw smoke rising. The pile had been set on fire. It was necessary to burn these extra supplies to keep the excited folk from taking their discarded belongings with them.

And now came another order. "Select the best handcarts. Leave all those with wobbly wheels. There will be one cart for two families from here on. Now get together and load the chosen carts quickly. Hurry, hurry. There are signs of a snowstorm. We must get over the mountains before the snow begins to fall."

George stood there unable to help. He was thinking of Aaron's words, "If I go, there will be one less to feed." Finally the boy said to himself, "I'm of no use. I will not go any farther with the handcarts."

He slipped away quietly into a thicket of willows that bordered Deer Creek. There he hid and watched until the last handcart had disappeared over the hill to the west. In the rush no one noticed the boy was missing.

George remembered that early in the day they had passed an Indian camp a little east of Deer Creek. Would those Indians help him get to his brother? He did not know, but he felt it was safer to take that chance than to go on being a burden to his parents. So he started back.

A mile or so along the trail he came to the tepees. As he neared one of them, he saw a boy about his size standing in front of it. Forgetting that he could not understand a word of English, George spoke to the young Indian. The boy looked at him and then turned suddenly and ducked into the tepee.

The starving white boy followed. Lifting the flap of elkskin at the opening, he saw the astonished Indian family—a mother and several children seated round a fire. On the embers was a kettle with something cooking in it.

Pointing to the kettle, George pleaded, "Give me some! Give me some!"

The mother understood. Reaching for a tin plate, she filled it with pieces of boiled buffalo meat. George seized it and began to eat ravenously.

When it was gone, he again handed the empty plate to the Indian mother, saying, "Give me some more! Give me some more!"

"Oo-oo!" she exclaimed in sympathy as she began to refill the plate.

The boy ate as hungrily as before. When he had finished the second helping, she motioned for him to leave. George tried to get up to go, but as he rose, he swooned and fell back on the buffalo robe.

The kind Indian mother bathed his face with

water until he finally opened his eyes. As George was too weak to stand up, there was nothing for the Indian family to do but to let him sleep in the tepee that night.

Somewhat refreshed next morning, he went outside and sat on a robe beside the tepee. Other Indian mothers, hearing that a starving white boy was in camp, came with food. Buffalo meat, venison and dog meat, which they considered a special treat, were brought to him.

George ate and ate. It seemed as if he could never have enough food.

But Jeff Baker, white husband of the kind Indian mother who had taken care of George the night before, warned him not to overeat. Too much at one time might kill him. Though George argued that he was still hungry, he took the man's advice and soon curled up and fell asleep.

The cool clear mountain air did much to restore him. And to his joy, when he awoke, he saw his father, tears running down his cheeks, bending over him.

"Thank the good Lord I have found you," he exclaimed.

"Oh, Father, these people have been so kind to me. They have saved my life. But how are Mother and my sisters?"

"They are well, but worried about you. Come, George, we must hurry to overtake them. We must be on our way at once."

"Are you trying to take the boy with you?" asked Baker. "Why, he can't walk! He can't possibly go."

"But what shall I do? His mother is crying for him. If he can't walk, I'll have to carry him," said brave Father Harrison.

"You can hardly carry yourself, man," was the quick answer. "Leave him here with us. We will take care of him and next year when he is strong again he can find a way to join you."

Father Harrison hesitated. He knew the

man spoke truly. George was in no shape to make the hard journey that lay ahead.

"What shall I do, George? Do you want to stay?"

"I'll be all right here, Father," answered George, "and next year I'll follow and find you in the valleys. Give my love to Mother and tell her not to worry."

"God bless you, son," said his father, and turning to the mountaineer, he added, "How can we ever thank you?"

"We're glad to help anyone in trouble. But before you leave you must have plenty to eat, and we'll give you some jerked buffalo meat to take with you. You'll need it."

Father Harrison was deeply moved. How kind these Indians were—and how generous, this white mountaineer!

"Good-by. God bless you all," said Father Harrison, as with a heart full of gratitude and renewed courage he set out to rejoin the band of handcart pioneers.

Through the Snow

"DID YOU FIND GEORGIE? Did you find him?" cried the anxious mother.

"Yes, Mother, I found him, but I had to leave him with some good friends." Then Father Harrison told them how kind the new-found Indian friends had been and that George was spending the winter with them. A good night's sleep brought the rest the father so sorely needed. By morning he was ready to face the problems that lay ahead.

How to cross the North Platte River was the first one. A toll bridge had been built over the stream, but its owner, used to getting high prices from gold-seekers rushing to California, asked more than the handcart company could pay. In spite of all they could do or say, he refused to accept less.

"Very well," declared one of the leaders. "We'll not be robbed of the little money we have. Come on, boys. The water is cold, but it's not too deep. Let's go through." And saying this, he led the men in fording the river. One after another the handcarts followed.

Mother Harrison, Mother Loader and the small children were taken across in one of the covered wagons—as were other mothers and children and those too ill to go through the water. Bob Loader and another boy drove the herd of cows. On the opposite bank the wagons waited, in case they were needed to help those struggling with the carts. For though the water was only waist-deep, the current was strong.

Suddenly, Mother Loader screamed, "Save my girls!"

The swift current was gradually carrying the cart with the girls downstream. In a flash

Lieutenant Tyler, loosing the lasso on his saddle, flung the end of it to the girls.

"Tie this to your shaft," he called. Struggling and trying for a foothold on the slippery rocks of the streambed, they managed at last to get the rope fastened. With the help of the men on the bank, the cart was slowly brought across. The girls, the contents of the carts, and the men who pushed and pulled were dripping, but all were safe and nothing else mattered.

To add to the discomfort of wet clothing, a cold wind arose, and with it a blinding snowstorm. All they could do was pitch camp and crawl under the half-raised tent until it blew over. By morning more than a foot of snow covered the forlorn and hungry band. But the sun shone clear and bright, and soon the dismal scene did not seem quite so discouraging.

"Come, come," called the Captain. "Get what food you can and then let us go on. We cannot stay here. We must push through the snow. Let the wagons break the way. The rest

of you must follow. Hard work will warm you up."

"No wagon for me," called Mother Loader. "Others need to ride worse than I do. They can take my place. Come, girls, let's get our cart moving." Her courage stirred others. Then Lieutenant Tyler was heard singing the hymn that had so often cheered the pioneers on their journey across the plains.

Voices were trembling and eyes filled with tears as the song rose along the line, but new strength seemed to come to them. Though the going was slow and hard, the caravan moved on until it neared the next camp ground on Willow Creek. Then came a stirring surprise!

Out of the mist on the snowy hill ahead came three horsemen—Joseph Young, Abe Garr and Dan Jones—couriers from a relief train. As they rode up and called that food and help were near, a glad cry rose all along the caravan.

"The Lord has not forgotten us," exclaimed

Father Harrison. "We shall get to Zion as we were promised."

The women and children laughed and talked. New life and cheer had come.

"Prepare for a square meal," spoke up Dan Jones, who was riding back with the Captain.

"I've been ready for two months," came a laughing answer.

What a feast at Willow Springs that night! They had earned this short time of rest and rejoicing.

The next morning, early, they made their way with new hope to Devil's Gate, where they were to be met by young teamsters from the valleys with wagons, food and bedding. Here the handcarts were to be left, and the rest of the trip through the South Pass down into the valleys of Utah was to be made in wagons.

When the leaders learned the handcart emigrants were in trouble, the rescue party had been quickly organized. Unfortunately, it did not reach the suffering people quickly enough to save them all. Many had died and been buried along the trail. But the hardy mountain boys managed to get most of them safely through. The brave handcart pioneers were rescued.

"How I wish that George and Aaron were with us," sighed Mother Harrison as they were welcomed into the warm home of one of the settlers.

"We all do," said Father Harrison. "But while we wait for them to rejoin us—and I have faith they will—we can make a home for them."

Tepee Days

AT FIRST, LIFE in the tepee was rather hard for young George. Jeff Baker was away much of the time and he had no one to talk to. The Indian mother did what she could to make him happy, and to build up his strength. The food she gave him was mostly meat—fresh, when she had it—but mainly jerked buffalo, for game was scarce. Once in a while she brought him dried berries. The food was nourishing and there was plenty of it. So George gradually grew stronger.

He and Jeff often talked of the days before they had gone west—Jeff, of his life in Kentucky, and George of his boyhood in England.

"It's not like England here, nor like old Kentucky," said Jeff, "but when you get used

53

to this mountain country, you won't want to leave it."

In time, George grew to like it, and the days passed pleasantly. He and little Tabi, the Indian boy who had first seen him, became great friends. (Tabi is Indian for "sun.") It didn't take long for them to learn to understand each other.

Tabi and George hunted rabbits, sage hens and other small game with bows and arrows. These, with an occasional trout which they caught, added to the family food supply.

Soon the Indian band moved to a warmer place for the winter. The tepee village was pitched in a sheltered place near a grove of tall trees. A stream of clear water ran near by, and patches of green grass supplied the ponies with fresh food. There was plenty of dry wood from the grove for cooking and for the fires, when cold winds and the "snowy" moon appeared.

The Indian women worked hard. Not only

did they do all the cooking, serving and attending to home duties, but they tanned the hides and prepared the skins of the antelope, deer, elk and buffalo the hunters brought in.

George liked to watch the Indian women at work. To tan a hide they first scalded it in boiling water. Then, after staking and stretching it on the ground, or between trees, they removed the hair with scraping knives. When the skin had been well worked over, and softened—sometimes with tallow rubbed into it —the skin was smoked over the fire, to give it a tawny shade.

Out of these skins the women made leggings, moccasins, gloves and shirts.

One day the Indian mother noticed that George's trousers were almost worn out so she went to work. A few days later she had not only made him some leggings, but a beaded buckskin shirt and moccasins that came above his ankles. The Indian children laughed to see him dressed like them. George was proud of his good-looking comfortable suit, and tried to show his gratitude by being helpful.

Indian ponies, grazing close to camp, brought some excitement to him and the other boys of the camp. The Indian boys had a chance to break those that had not been ridden. George thought he would like to try riding one. His only experience with horses was when he and Bob had driven the cow herd of the handcart caravan. He chose a shaggy, sleepy pony for the first venture. With the help of his pal, he got a rawhide loop into the little animal's mouth, and managed to mount it. But before he was fairly seated, the pony began to buck and George was pitched over its head into a bank of soft snow. He came out unhurt except for his pride. It was the last of his "Injun pony rides."

However, there really was not much fun for the white boy round the Indian camp. During the winter months the days were spent inside the tepees for the most part. There

were no books to read, no pictures to see.
Occasionally Jeff told interesting experiences of
his trapping, hunting, or fighting rival Indian
tribes.

Some of the children went out and had fun
sliding on the ice or down the snowy hills.
They broke holes in the ice and caught fish
that came up for the bait. And sometimes they
trapped muskrats and other small animals.
George was glad to join with them. It was a
change. But in spite of all these different
pastimes, he was homesick and longed to get
back to his own family. When the day came
that the tepee village was taken down, and the
Indian band set out on the trail again, George's
heart jumped for joy.

Back to Fort Laramie

SPRING HAD COME and the Indians were breaking camp for a trek to the trading post. George
didn't know where they were going, and Jeff
didn't say. There was much packing to be
done. The family used two travois, several
pack ponies and even a few dogs with travois,
to take the camp outfit, the buckskins and
other things they had to trade.

Failure to learn to ride Injun ponies made the
trip a hard one for George. Walking reminded
him of the handcart journey. He was thankful
to be well enough to keep up. Sometimes he
was even ahead of the Indian caravan.

One afternoon as he waited for the Indians
to catch up with him, George thought he
would freeze to death. He was on a bleak hill.

An icy wind, carrying snow from drifts along the crest, cut his face. His buckskin shirt, leggings and moccasins did not keep out the piercing cold. Besides, he was wet from wading through snowdrifts that lay across the trail. It seemed the band would never get there. To keep warm he ran back and forth on a bare spot along the hillside. He was so sleepy he wanted to lie down and take a nap, but he remembered what Jeff had told him. "If you go to sleep when you are freezing cold, you may never wake up." He didn't dare give in so he kept moving about until the band finally arrived. After that he remembered not to get too far ahead of them.

Camp was made in a grove of aspens at the foot of a hill where it was much warmer. The tepees were soon put up. Fires were built and the supper eaten. The meat tasted good though it was only half cooked. As he lay in his warm buffalo robes, George forgot all his troubles of the afternoon. He was comfortable.

The Indians were about twenty "sleeps" (nights) on the trail. Where they were heading, George still did not know. He only knew they were going to a white man's trading post. Every morning he got up early to help with the packing and all day he and his Indian pal stayed at the head of the caravan.

Then one evening, just at sunset, Tabi, who had raced ahead to the top of a hill, signaled to George to hurry and join him. There, in the valley below, was Fort Laramie, the Stars and Stripes waving above it. George suddenly realized that soon he would see his brother Aaron. His heart bounded with happiness.

The tepees were pitched that night by the Laramie River. When the ponies had been turned out to graze on the good grasses along the stream, and the supper of broiled antelope was over, George was allowed to go into the Post to hunt for his brother.

What a surprise for both of them! What a joyous visit they had that evening! Neither had heard a word of their family nor of each other since the parting six months before.

Mail service wasn't well developed in the West in those days. Letters were occasionally passed along the trail in covered wagons. But none of these wagons traveled over the Rockies during the winter months.

Mountain men had brought word to Fort Laramie of the tragic suffering of the handcart company, but Aaron could not tell how many nor who had perished. Of course, the brothers were anxious to hear from their family, but there was no news.

Aaron hadn't heard that George had gone off with the Indians and he eagerly listened to all George told him. He could see that his brother was sturdy and had been well treated.

"You certainly don't look like the boy who left here six months ago," said Aaron.

"You are looking pretty husky yourself, Aaron," replied George. "A soldier's life must be all right." And so the boys talked! There were so many things each wanted to know.

The bugle call put an end to their visit. Aaron had to turn in and George to go back to his Indian friends. Goodnights were said, and George hurried back to the lodge. But early next morning he was again at the Fort, this time with Tabi.

Bugles were sounding.

"Do you mind if we watch the soldiers drill?" asked George of one of the guards.

"Sure not. Suit yourself," he said, with a grin.

For half an hour the boys sat on the steps of one of the barracks, wide-eyed with interest as the soldiers went through their maneuvers. Drill over, Aaron found them. After showing them around the Fort, he want back with them to the tepee village. Jeff Baker was friendly. He told Aaron how he had first found George and how he had persuaded their father to let George stay with the Indians.

At the invitation of Aaron's sergeant,

George had dinner with his brother. How good it seemed—after months of Indian food—to taste flapjacks, bacon and beans, with a bit of jam to top off the meal.

Much to his delight, George learned that Tom Blakely, who was going to the Missouri River for some freight, would need a boy to do the chores for his wife while he was away, and might take him. The thought of getting a job near Aaron seemed almost too good to be true. George went right away to inquire and to his joy was hired to begin work the next morning. It was agreed that he was to live at the Blakely home—a three-room cabin just outside the fort.

George tried not to show how happy he was when he told his Indian mother of his plans. She took the news sadly, and the children cried when he left.

But George promised to come to see them and before they left the Indians visited him at the cabin. Mrs. Blakely made the children happy with cookies and trinkets. She gave the mother a piece of bright calico, while George gave Tabi a pocket knife Aaron had given him. These were simple gifts, but they made his friends happy. A few days later the Indian band took the trail westward again to spend the summer in the mountains.

When Tom Blakely returned with the freight train, George had another job waiting for him. Dr. Getty, a physician and surgeon in the army, hired the boy to cook for him. It was just the work George wanted. Although he hadn't had much practice beyond helping the cook on the *Horizon* flip pancakes, he had always been interested in cooking.

From his Indian mother he learned to cook trout, buffalo, antelope and deer roasts. So when he had to prepare food for the Doctor, he remembered not only what he had seen her do, but some of the things he had learned from his own mother.

Dr. Getty lived upstairs in one of the buildings reserved for officers. In another part of the same quarters lived a colonel with his wife and daughters. Fortunately for George the Colonel had an Englishman for a cook. Since George came from England, the colonel's cook took a special interest in him. Often when young George was trying to get a meal for the Doctor, the cook would slip over into the kitchen and help him, giving him many good ideas on what to do as well as on how to do it.

Aaron and George saw each other often. As summertime approached, oxtrains from the West began to arrive at the fort. The teamsters brought the first real news of the Harrison family. They said that all had stood the hardships of getting through the snow and over the mountains. This news made the boys more anxious than ever to join their folks in the valley.

That summer another experience brought back pleasant memories of the handcart days. A band of young Mormons had been called to mission fields in the East and in Europe. They had little money and, like the Harrisons, traveled on foot over the same trail. And as they walked they sang:

> For some must push and some must pull
> Before we reach our mission, O!

One night they camped just outside of Fort Laramie. Aaron and George, anxious for news of their family, got permission to visit them. The boys were welcomed and from the young men had still more news of their family and friends. They stayed up late that evening, talking over their experiences and singing the songs they had known in England.

Next morning as Aaron and George watched the missionaries filing merrily down the Platte along the trail that had been such a tragic one for them not many months before, their desire to get on to the valleys grew stronger than ever.

On to Fort Bridger

IN MARCH 1858, the commander at Fort Laramie was ordered to Fort Bridger, about four hundred miles west across the Rockies. He was to take supplies to Johnston's army, for the troops at Bridger were on less than half rations.

Dr. Getty, who was to accompany the relief train, took George with him. The weather was cold and raw, even worse than the March before when George was returning with the Indians to Fort Laramie. And then the snow came. For several days they were unable to move. The cold grew more and more intense. Though the men were able to keep warm, the mules and horses suffered pitifully. All they had to eat was bark from trees the soldiers had cut down, and small portions of grain that

69

could be brought along. Some of the poor animals froze to death.

When the train finally reached Horseshoe Bend, after the delay in the snow, George saw that some Indians had made camp at this point. Thinking they might be his friends or perhaps have news of them, he went over to the tepees. Sure enough! It was the Indian mother and her family. Jeff and Tabi were away. They had gone to hunt game.

A shout of joy greeted the white boy. The children hugged his legs and danced with glee. The Indian mother, though glad to see him, seemed troubled. Finally she told him she could give him nothing to eat. They were without any food. They were all hungry.

This was almost more than George could bear. He remembered how generously she had shared her food with him when he went to her tepee.

"I'll do what I can for you," he said, as he hastened back to Dr. Getty.

"Doctor," he began, "there's an Indian family across the creek, starving. It's the same one that saved my life when I left the handcart company. I must get some food for them."

"I am sorry, deeply sorry, but you know we have been put on half rations to help Johnston's troops. I don't think I can do a thing for you."

"But I must have it," George pleaded. "They may starve. Won't you please get the quartermaster to let you have some food? You can take it out of my wages."

"It isn't a question of money," said the Doctor. "You could have food in a minute if there was any to spare. I'm afraid even I can't help you."

George couldn't stand it. He began to cry.

The Doctor was troubled. He didn't like to disappoint George. But what could he do? Telling the boy not to be too upset, that he would do what he could, Dr. Getty went to the quartermaster's tent. How he got the food, George never knew, but he was soon back with a sack full of bacon, beans, flour and a little sugar. It wasn't much but it would help.

The boy thanked him warmly and ran straight to the Indian camp. George felt it was small pay for what the Indians had done for him. It pleased him to be able to show his gratitude.

George visited with the grateful Indians until time for "taps." As he was leaving, the children cried and begged him to stay. The Indian mother gave him a pair of beaded moccasins which he treasured. George managed to get a little more food for them before he left for the West. Then he had to say a final good-by.

He hated to leave them and worried about the family. Fortunately, he met Jeff and Tabi on the trail. They were returning to Horseshoe Bend with two fat deer on their pack ponies. George had them meet Dr. Getty. He told them how the Doctor had helped him to get food for the family.

They visited together a little while. Then

as Jeff left he said, "Hope you'll come back, boy. Remember—our tepee is always home for you. Good luck to you."

"Good luck to you and your family," answered George. "You've been mighty good to me, and I'll never forget it."

That was the last he ever saw of these people, but George always remembered them with gratitude.

After leaving Jeff and Tabi, George went with the relief train along the same trail the handcarts had taken nearly two years before. At Deer Creek he saw the ashes of the big bonfire in which they had burned their precious possessions.

At Devil's Gate he saw the stone fort with a few broken handcarts still lying about. From there it was a steady climb up the pleasant Sweetwater Valley to the South Pass—a wide almost level way over the crest of the continent. They followed down the gentle slopes along streams that led to the Green River.

They still had about a hundred miles farther to travel to Fort Bridger, but finally reached there. The soldiers, who had spent a cold, hungry winter in the Fort, were glad to see the relief train rolling in with supplies of food. Extra rations were issued at once. It was good to have plenty to eat once more.

Dr. Getty, who had received orders to remain at the Fort, wanted George to stay with him. But the boy was so eager to see his parents and sisters that he couldn't stay away any longer.

The Doctor understood and didn't blame him. He paid his young cook for the eight and a half months he had served him—ten dollars a month and board. The Doctor counted out the money—eight ten dollar pieces and one five dollar piece—in gold! George thanked him warmly. How rich he felt!

Then the Doctor arranged for George to cook for a captain and a lieutenant who were with Johnston's troops. George was happy to get this job, and the chance of going on with them to the valley.

But what was he to do with all his money? That was a real problem. He had no place to keep his savings. If some of the soldiers knew he had money, they would want to borrow it, and perhaps lose it at cards.

George finally went to Lieutenant Bumstead, whom he had often met at Dr. Getty's quarters, and asked if he would do him a favor. Surprised, the lieutenant questioned George and to his amusement learned that he was the only officer to whom George would entrust his gold. The lieutenant, pleased with the boy's confidence, finally agreed to act as his banker. George felt greatly relieved when he handed over his hard-earned money.

The Promised Valley

IT WAS A JOYOUS DAY for George when the soldiers and he left Fort Bridger for the valleys of Utah. Aaron was going with his company. After a delay of two years the brothers looked forward to a happy reunion with their father. mother, and sisters.

Over the hills and across the rim of the Great Basin the soldiers marched into colorful Echo Canyon. They climbed the "Big Mountain" of Wasatch range. From the top of this ridge, they could see the Promised Valley.

The army marched through Salt Lake City until they reached Cedar Valley, the place selected for the army post. The post, named Camp Floyd in honor of John Floyd, Secretary of War in President Buchanan's cabinet, was built on an oasis in the desert, about forty miles southwest of Salt Lake City.

Aaron was kept busy with drilling and guard duties most of the time while George did the cooking for the officers. They didn't have time to walk the forty miles to Springville, where the family had settled, but as soon as Father Harrison heard of their arrival he was not long in getting to Camp Floyd to see his sons.

It was a joyful meeting. There was so much to talk about. George could hardly wait to introduce his father to the lieutenant who had kept his gold for him all this time.

After a cordial greeting and introduction, the boy asked the lieutenant if he might have his money.

"Certainly," said the officer.

It was a proud moment for George when he handed over the eighty-five dollars he had saved so carefully. As for Father Harrison, the surprise and pleasure were almost more than he could bear. His eyes filled with tears as he embraced his son, and tried to thank him.

"You can, indeed, be proud of George," said Lieutenant Bumstead. "There are not many boys who could have worked as hard, or saved their wages as carefully as George has done."

With this money Father Harrison bought oxen which he greatly needed to work his farm. Duties kept Aaron and George for a time at Camp Floyd, but they were finally given leave to visit their family.

What a joyful reunion there was at the new cabin home in the West, with Mother and the happy sisters clustered around the brothers, and the proud father looking on!

"Why, Olive and Alice, you have grown!" exclaimed George.

"Baby Martha too," said Alice. "See, she can walk."

"Is this the tiny one who rode on the handcart?" asked Aaron, lifting the shy, smiling little girl.

Hours flew until the boys had to return to the frontier post.

Not many months passed before Camp Floyd was abandoned. Then, with honorable discharge, Aaron and George went home to work on the farm, and to help, as youthful pioneers, in developing a prosperous American town in the beautiful valley.

In time, young George married, and had a home of his own in Springville, Utah. On the main road, near the Wasatch Mountains, he built a hotel which, as the "Harrison House" was to become famous throughout the country. And because of the fine food he served and his excellent cooking, George, the handcart boy, became the well-known "Beefsteak Harrison." In spite of his success and fame, George never forgot the long, weary, hungry days he had experienced on the road to the Promised Valley —to Zion, land of the free.

ᘯ☙

Historical Information

Howard R. Driggs

Howard Roscoe Driggs was the son and grandson of Utah pioneers whose stories inspired in him a lifelong passion of finding and preserving firsthand stories of pioneers of the American West. He knew George "Beefsteak" Harrison, heard him tell his story, and published it as George the Handcart Boy.

Dr. Driggs was born August 8, 1873, in Pleasant Grove, Utah. He began his schooling in West Jordan, Utah, and later attended and taught in the public schools of Pleasant Grove. He graduated from the University of Utah Normal School in 1897, received a Bachelor of Arts degree from the University

83

of Utah in 1908 and a Master of Arts degree in 1918.

His teaching career in Utah and New York State spanned a period of over 50 years. In 1897, he began teaching English at the Branch Normal School (now Southern Utah University) in Cedar City, Utah, and later was an instructor in English at the University of Utah. His role of one of the founding faculty at Southern Utah University was taken in to consideration when SUU acquired his papers and publications in 2004 and created the Howard R. Driggs Collection in the Sherratt Library Special Collections & Archives.

He moved to New York City as a visiting professor of English Education at New York University, where he received his doctoral degree in 1926 and taught until his retirement in 1942. He wrote two series of textbooks for English teachers, Live Language Lessons and Living English. In the 1920s and 1930s he was co-author and editor of a number of books in the Pioneer Life Series, published by World Book Company. One of these books was Ox-Team Days on the Oregon Trail, on which he collaborated with Ezra Meeker, a well-known Oregon Trail pioneer. Meeker later formed the Oregon Trail Memorial Association (OTMA) and served as its first president. Driggs became president after Meeker's death in 1928. The name of the association changed in 1941 to the American Pioneer Trails Association, which Dr. Driggs headed until his death in 1963.

He wrote and edited over 50 books, many of them to interest students in the history of the American West which he loved.

J. Rulon Hales

J. Rulon Hales, who illustrated George, the Handcart Boy, was a close friend and associate of Howard R. Driggs in New York City where he had a career as a successful commercial artist. Hales was born 8 March 1899 in Rexburg, Idaho. He married Vera Marie Holbrook of Bountiful, Utah, in 1923, and they moved to New York City where he worked as an illustrator on many national advertising campaigns. They raised three children, Gerald, Janet and Robert D. Hales died in Utah in 1986.

For the American Pioneer Trails Association, he produced a map of the

Mormon Trail Route in 1947, and illustrated these books: *George, The Handcart Boy; A Western Cowkid: On Trails and Ranches of the West; When Grandfather Was A Boy; Mormon Trail: The Pathway of Pioneers Who Made Deserts Bloom; Timpanogos Town; Driggs Family History: Book One; Money Rock: A Drama of the Pony Express;* and the pamphlet *New Light on Old Glory: Our Star-Spangled Banner In Its Historic Setting* all by Howard R. Driggs.

George Harrison

George Harrison walked across the United States from Iowa to Wyoming in a pioneer handcart company when he was 14 years old, but his story ended much differently than most pioneer boys. It was written and published by Howard R. Driggs who knew him fifty years later when he ran the famous Harrison Hotel in Springville at the turn of the 20th century.

George was born in Manchester, Lancashire, England, in 1841 to William and Hannah Harrison. In 1842 they became converts to The Church of Jesus Christ of Latter-day Saints. By 1856 they were the parents of five boys and five girls, although three infant boys died in England. William, Hannah, and their seven remaining children joined a large company that was emigrating from England on the ship Horizon. It left Liverpool on May 25, 1856 bound for Boston, and eventually the Great Salt Lake Valley where the Latter-day Saints were gathering.

George was the second oldest son. His siblings were a brother, Aaron (18), and five sisters, Mary Ann (12) Alice (10) Olivia (7), Hannah (almost 2) and a baby Sarah Ellen (5 months). Early in the trek, George helped Aaron pull their handcarts, but he and some other boys got the "chills and fever" from swimming in a slough thick with mosquitoes. George had to be taken into one of the wagons carrying the company's extra supplies. He was sick and weak and considered himself a burden to the family, especially as the rations were reduced in October. He left the wagon train on October 17th, thinking he might go

to Fort Laramie where Aaron had stayed to join the Army. But instead he found an Indian camp where he remained and was nursed back to health. The Indians called him "white skeleton boy," and he stayed until spring with them. The camp moved east and one day he and an Indian pal ran ahead to the top of a hill. When they reached the top, there in the valley below was old Fort Laramie. He later wrote, "Above it, in the golden rays of the setting sun waved the Stars and Stripes. It was the prettiest sight of my life."

He became a cook's helper in Johnston's Army, and eventually marched with the army through Great Salt Lake City after the pioneers and the Army leaders agreed to let them camp thirty miles from Salt Lake City. He remained a cook until Camp Floyd was abandoned at the outbreak of the Civil War in 1861. He not only opened a restaurant and a hotel, but entertained his guests with song and prose. He was the ward chorister for many years and sang with a quartet for many decades. If he knew anyone was ill, he would send a bucket of soup to help the patient. It was said that "he had given enough soup away to 'float him right to heaven.'" He married Rosella D. White and they had ten children. He died in Springville on February 2, 1921.

Martin Handcart Company

The William Harrison family traveled from England in 1856 with a large company of Latter-day Saint emigrants. This was the fifth largest pioneer company to leave in the spring of 1856, as there were many hundreds of Latter-day Saint converts anxious to travel "Zion." It was very late in the season to start such a venture. They traveled across the Atlantic on the ship Horizon, reaching Boston on June 30 after a voyage of 35 days. The company traveled by train to Iowa City, Iowa, for eight to ten days, and then learned that they would have to wait another three weeks. The four earlier companies had taken all the handcarts and new handcarts had to be made from unseasoned wood which resulted in additional delays and repairs on the trail.

Several companies had successfully crossed the plains of America by handcart, but George's family and others faced continual difficulties. There were 576 people who left Iowa City on July 28, with 146 carts, 7 wagons, 30 oxen, and 50 cows and beef cattle. Their hastily built carts had to be repaired frequently which caused more delays near Omaha, Nebraska. A few people took refuge there, but the Martin Handcart Company, named after its leader Elder Edward Martin, left Florence on August 25. It took almost five weeks to go 500 miles across Nebraska. By October 8, they were at Fort Laramie where they expected to find additional provisions. There were none, so their food rations were cut, and they forged ahead.

Because of their growing weakness, they decided to lighten the loads they were pulling, so they discarded blankets and clothing. (George said they put on their best clothes and burned their old ones to make the handcarts easier to pull.) On October 19 they crossed the North Platte River. As soon as they crossed, it started to snow. Several people died that night. These early winter storms and cold temperatures continued. The men became so weak and sick they couldn't pitch the tents. Twelve miles beyond the river crossing, they were stopped in the deep snow. Fifty-six had died.

Early in October President Brigham Young heard there were still pioneers on the trail. Knowing they would have problems, he called for many volunteers to go to their aid. Horsemen, wagons, and supplies were sent. On October 28, three men from the rescue party rode into the camp of the Martin Company. The deep snow had halted the rescue wagons, so the men told the emigrants their only hope was to keep moving to reach the rescue wagons. They struggled on, and on November 3, they met the first of the supply wagons at Horse Creek. The rescuers urged the company to move on and find better shelter from the snow and cold. The company pushed on until they came to the Sweetwater River. For many, crossing the river seemed more than they could manage, but men from the rescue party bravely carried the pioneers across and they found shelter in a mountain cove.

When they moved on, they left most of the handcarts behind. The rescuers loaded the sickest and weakest into wagons, but the rest had to walk. After a break in the storms, it began snowing again, but by November 19, there were enough wagons for all to ride the rest of the way into the valley. They finally reached Salt Lake on November 30. About 145 people had lost their lives on the way. All the members of the William Harrison family lived to reach the Salt Lake Valley, but baby Sarah Ellen died about four months later in March 1857. In February 1858, another baby girl, Martha Ann, joined the family in Springville where they had settled.

www.ingramcontent.com/pod-product-compliance
Lightning Source LLC
LaVergne TN
LVHW021540080426
835509LV00019B/2757